TIME
FOR KIDS

Craft It:
Hand-Blown
GLASS

Madison Spielman

Consultant

Timothy Rasinski, Ph.D.
Kent State University

Publishing Credits

Dona Herweck Rice, *Editor-in-Chief*
Robin Erickson, *Production Director*
Lee Aucoin, *Creative Director*
Conni Medina, M.A.Ed., *Editorial Director*
Jamey Acosta, *Editor*
Stephanie Reid, *Photo Editor*
Rachelle Cracchiolo, M.S.Ed., *Publisher*

Based on writing from *TIME For Kids*.

TIME For Kids and the *TIME For Kids* logo are registered trademarks of TIME Inc. Used under license.

Teacher Created Materials

5301 Oceanus Drive
Huntington Beach, CA 92649-1030
http://www.tcmpub.com

ISBN 978-1-4333-3619-5

© 2012 by Teacher Created Materials, Inc.

BP 5028

Table of Contents

History of Glassblowing

Glassblowing is a very old art. It began about four thousand years ago in Mesopotamia (mehs-uh-puh-TAY-mee-uh).

Glassblowing is blowing air into liquid glass to shape it.

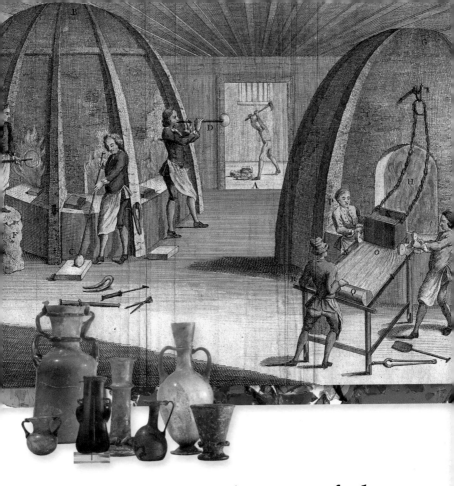

The first popular use of glass was in ancient Rome. This is because the first metal pipe for blowing glass was invented in Rome. The Romans were able to make glass easily and skillfully.

A New World of Glass

Glassblowing was one of the first businesses in the New World. Captain John Smith brought **gaffers** from Europe.

Gaffers are glassblowers.
They built their factory near the
sandy shores of Jamestown.

glassblowing—long ago

More people knew how
to blow glass in the past than
people know how to do so today.

glassblowing—today

But modern gaffers still blow glass in much of the same way gaffers did long ago.

Glassblowing has not changed much over time.

Modern gaffers still use tools very much like those the Romans used.

Glassblowing Now

The main things glassblowers need to make glass are sand, lime, soda ash, potash, and very high heat.

potash	
sodium carbonate (soda ash)	
lime	
sand	

Chemicals are sometimes used to add different colors to glass.

How do sand, lime, soda ash and potash become something made of glass? Read on to find out.

The ingredients are mixed together and heated.

Today, a gas **furnace** (FUR-nis) is used to make the high heat. In the past, very hot wood fires were built in brick ovens.

A furnace is an oven used to melt glass. The heat used to make glass is very high. The oven has a special screen for protection.

When the temperature is high enough, the ingredients melt together to make liquid glass.

Gaffers must be very careful not to burn themselves!

The gaffer picks up a small amount of glass on the end of a **blowpipe**. This is called a **gather**.

Then the gather is rolled against a smooth, flat table or paddle. This shapes the glass and cools it down a bit.

Next, the gaffer blows into the blowpipe to make a bubble. The bubble size depends on the size of the object the gaffer wants to make.

The gaffer keeps reheating the glass, blowing into it, and shaping it.

There are plenty of tools to help the gaffer do this. Molds and scissors are two of them. The gaffer can also sit in a special chair. It has long arms to help hold the blowpipe.

Soon the piece of glass
begins to take shape.

tweezers

paddle

A paddle and other tools are used to get the shape just right.

Stems, handles, and other pieces can be added to the glass with more gathers.

The annealing kiln heats and cools the glass slowly to make it sturdy.

The last step is cooling the glass. Glass cooled too quickly will shatter. So the gaffer puts it in a special **kiln** for one or more days.

Hand-Blown Art

In the past, blown glass was usually made into things for everyday use like bowls or dishes. Today, some hand-blown glass is still used that way. But much of it is art.

Art shops and museums are filled with beautiful pieces of hand-blown glass. They are true works of art!

Glossary

blowpipe

furnace

gaffers

gather

kiln